Folens
RE in Action 3

Susan Smart

Introduction

Year Three
This book is intended to fit very closely to the QCA schemes of work in RE. There are five units within the Year Three schemes. These are:

Unit 3A – What do signs and symbols mean in religion?
Unit 3B – How and why do Hindus celebrate Divali?
Unit 3C – What do we know about Jesus?
Unit 3D – What is the Bible and why is it important for Christians?
Unit 3E – What is faith and what difference does it make?

In each unit there will be a focus upon the following objectives:

Unit 3A
Noah's ark
Seder meal
Metaphors
God
Symbols in a church

Unit 3B
Rama and Sita
Celebrating Divali
Lakshmi

Unit 3C
Jesus
What was Jesus like?

Unit 3D
Mary Jones
Old Testament/New Testament
Bible writing

Unit 3E
Hagar
Sarah
Abraham

This book provides detailed teacher notes and suggested activities based on the QCA schemes of work. Each QCA unit is expected to cover half a term's work and six hours of lessons. The materials within the book cover many of the learning objectives within each QCA unit. They build on knowledge and skills acquired in previous years.

Each unit of work in the book includes a page of teacher notes, which provides the knowledge required to teach the lesson. There then follows a starting point for discussion and two or three differentiated activities that relate to or introduce the worksheets, which link specifically to the learning objectives included in the QCA units.

Photocopiable worksheets are provided to enable the pupils to complete the activities. The plenary is intended to review the information learned in the lesson.

Noah's ark

Learning objectives

Children should:
- think about the meaning of everyday signs and symbols
- explore meanings in stories.

Background

God saw that the people on earth were not behaving as He expected them to and He was very sad. However, there was one good man called Noah. God told Noah that He had decided that He was going to kill every man and woman that He had created but that He wanted Noah and his family to survive.

He instructed Noah to build an ark, into which he was to put his family and some animals. As soon as Noah, his family and the animals were safely in the ark, then God would send a flood.

Noah began to build the ark as God had told him to. His three sons helped. It took a long time but when the ark was finished, God sent a male and female of every animal and bird. The door to the ark closed as soon as everyone was safely on board. Then God sent the flood.

Soon the ark was floating upon the deep waters. All the animals and people who were not safely in the ark drowned. The rain didn't stop until the highest mountains were covered.

After several months, the rain stopped and the water level started to drop. The ark eventually came to rest on the mountain of Ararat. Noah sent out a bird to see how much of the earth was still covered. When the dove returned with an olive branch in its beak, Noah knew that it was nearly time to leave the ark.

God promised that He would never destroy the world again even though He knew that people would not always behave as they should. He told Noah and his family that if it ever rained for a long time again and they were worried He would break His promise, they should look up to the sky and they would see a rainbow there. This would be a sign that He would keep his promise.

Activities

Starting points	Discuss what we mean by a promise. Why is it important that we keep them? What happens if we break them?
Worksheet 1 (Easy) *'Noah'*	Ask the children if they can remember anyone else that they have learned about who was given an important job to do by God.
Worksheet 2 (Core) *'Promises'*	Talk about a time when someone broke a promise that they had made to you. Share with the children your feelings when it happened.
Worksheet 3 (Challenge) *'Noah's ark'*	Recap the main events of the story with the children and then ask them to retell the story in their own words.

Plenary

Consider God's actions with the children. Was He right to behave in the way that He did? Why do you think He decided to drown all the animals and people?

Noah

- Write a short description of Noah. Think about what sort of person he must have been for God to ask him to do such an important job. What qualities did he have? Was he reliable, honest or hard-working?

_____

_____

_____

_____

_____

_____

_____

_____

Promises

● Think about the promises that you have made, either to friends or family. Think about a time when you have made a promise you kept and a time when you broke a promise. How did the people affected feel when this happened?

A promise I kept...

I kept a promise when...

_____

_____

_____

_____

_____

A promise I broke...

I broke a promise when...

_____

_____

_____

_____

_____

Noah's ark

- Retell the story of Noah's Ark. Try to remember the main parts of the story.

Seder meal

Learning objectives

Children should:
- learn about the significance of Passover and its practice for Judaism
- understand how symbolic food can be used to remember important events
- reflect upon important events in their own lives.

Background

Passover is celebrated to remind Jews of when they escaped from their lives of slavery in Egypt. After the ten plagues, the leader of the Egyptians had agreed to let the Jewish slaves go. They left in such a hurry that there was no time to let their bread rise and it baked in the baskets on their shoulders. Jews will only eat unleavened bread (which has the special name of matzah) at Passover.

During Passover, families gather for the special meal and ceremony. The story of the Exodus from Egypt is read from a special book called the Haggadah.

The Seder meal is a special meal that is eaten at the time of the Jewish festival of Passover. It is important because each food included on the plate reminds Jews of when they lived their lives in slavery.
The foods on the Seder plate have special meanings. They are:
A roasted shank bone of lamb – burned and scorched to represent the sacrifice of the lambs before the Israelites left Egypt.
Hard-boiled egg – this represents the Temple offering.
Charoset – represents the mortar used by the Israelites in Egypt to make bricks.
Bitter herbs – represents the bitterness of Egyptian slavery.
Parsley, lettuce and green herbs – to remind Jews of spring time and new growth and hope. The greens are dipped in salt water to represent the tears of the children of Israel during their years in slavery.

Activities

Starting points	Talk about what feelings the Jews would have experienced at having to leave their homes.
Worksheet 4 (Mixed ability) *'Passover card'*	Think about all the other religious festivals that are celebrated by sending cards to one another and about all the different designs of card (religious, serious, humorous, and so on).
Worksheet 5 (Challenge) *'Feelings'*	Discuss how different feelings are experienced at different times. Which events in our lives cause happiness and which cause sadness?

Plenary

Ask the children to consider why Jews remember Passover.

Passover card

- Design a card for a Jewish family celebrating Passover. You may want to include some of the Jewish symbols shown on the worksheet.

The Seder plate: used during the celebration of Passover.

The Magen David: symbol of the Jewish faith.

The Haggadah: which contains the story of the Exodus from Egypt.

Feelings

● Describe a time when you may have had to do something, or when something may have happened, which caused distress. It could be the death of a family pet, moving house or moving school. How did things eventually improve?

Metaphors

Learning objectives

Children should:
- understand that words can have literal and non-literal meanings
- learn how to interpret religious metaphors.

Background

Metaphors are used when a writer writes about something as if it is really something else.

Examples of metaphors include:
- You're driving me up the wall.
- It's raining cats and dogs.
- Sorry, I must fly.

Metaphors can also be used on greeting cards: for example, 'Sorry you're under the weather.'

Metaphors are used in the Bible. Examples of biblical metaphors include:
- God is my rock (Psalm ch18 v2).
- Jesus is the light of the world (John ch8 v12).
- The Lord is my shepherd (Psalm 23).

Activities

Starting points	Discuss the religious metaphor, 'God is my rock' with the children. Ask the children to consider why Christians may use this metaphor when thinking of God. Then display a list of adjectives associated with this metaphor on the board.
Worksheet 6 (Easy) *'Metaphors'*	Ask the children to think about all the metaphors discussed so far. Have they heard of any others? Make a list of all the metaphors and number them.
Worksheet 7 (Mixed ability) *'When I'm...'*	Explore a range of feelings with the children. Consider what images each feeling creates?

Plenary

Try to think of other religious metaphors. What other metaphors would sum up the type of person that Jesus was and what he means to Christians?

Metaphors

● Choose two of the metaphors that your teacher has spoken about. Draw pictures to represent each metaphor, making sure that when your teacher marks your work, they know which metaphor it is from your picture!

Metaphor number 1

Metaphor number 2

When I'm...

● Explore a feeling such as jealousy, anger, greed or fear. An example is, 'When I'm angry, I feel like a balloon about to burst.' Write your own metaphor with a partner and illustrate it.

God

Learning objectives

Children should:
■ understand that symbolic language is used to describe God
■ learn that religious beliefs and ideas about God can be experienced in a variety of forms.

Background

Many religions expect their followers to behave in a certain way. These ways differ between each religion and sometimes within each religion. However, many religions believe in an absolute power or being, which is commonly known as God.

Hinduism
Hindus believe that there is one supreme God, called Brahman. Hindus believe that Brahman can be represented and thought about in many different forms. This shows the power and presence of God, who is believed to be everywhere. Hindus have thousands of gods and goddesses. Each god or goddess has his or her own characteristics. Three gods form what is known as the Trimurti: Vishnu, Shiva and Brahma. Brahma is the creator, Vishnu is the preserver and Shiva, the destroyer and re-creator.

Islam
Muslims believe that the word of God was revealed to a man called Muhammad (pbuh) in the early seventh century. Muhammad (pbuh) became known as the final prophet and the messenger of God. Islam means obedience to the will of Allah. Allah is the Arabic word for God. Throughout his life, Muhammad (pbuh) continued to receive messages from God through the Angel Jibril. The Qur'an, the Muslim holy book, teaches that God is in control of everything that happens and that Muslims should follow the will of Allah rather than following an individual path through life.

Judaism
Jews believe in one God. They believe that God made a promise to Abraham (known as the father of the Jewish people), called the covenant, in which God chose the Hebrews to be his special people with a responsibility to keep all his Commandments.

Jews do not write the name of God, as they believe it to be so holy. Instead, they write it in the form of YHVH. Jews follow the Ten Commandments, which form part of the greater 613 laws that were given in a renewed covenant during the Jews' time in the desert.

Activities

Starting points	Discuss God within Christianity. What beliefs do Christians have about their God?
Worksheet 8 (Easy) *'A Hindu god'*	Look at pictures of Hindu gods and goddesses. What do the children notice about them? Ask the children to draw their own Hindu god on the worksheet.
Worksheet 9 (Core) *'Questions'*	Discuss where we can find out more about the religions we have looked at and the views that believers have of the gods or God within Hinduism, Islam or Judaism.
Worksheet 10 (Challenge) *'Similarities and differences'*	Explore the reasons why different religions have different and similar beliefs about the gods or God they worship.

Plenary

Ask the group that completed the easy activity to show the gods and goddesses they have drawn. Can the other children guess from the pictures what qualities the deities may possess?

A Hindu god

- Imagine that you can create your own god in Hinduism. Draw a picture of your god and label him or her with adjectives. Think about the qualities that your god has and try to show some of these qualities in your picture. For example, if he was a kind god, he may have a smiling face.

FOLENS RE IN ACTION 3

© Folens (copiable page)

Questions

● Write a list of questions that you would like to be able to ask God if He were with you today.

1. _____

   _____

   _____

2. _____

   _____

   _____

3. _____

   _____

   _____

4. _____

   _____

   _____

Similarities and differences

- Think about how God is thought of in the religions of Judaism and Hinduism. Use some non-fiction books to help you. List the similarities and differences in the tables below.

Similarities	
Hinduism	**Judaism**
_____	_____
_____	_____
_____	_____
_____	_____
_____	_____

Differences	
Hinduism	**Judaism**
_____	_____
_____	_____
_____	_____
_____	_____
_____	_____

Symbols in a church

Learning objective

Children should:
■ learn about some common symbols in a place of worship.

Background

Symbols are very important in religion. In every place of worship we find symbols which signify special meanings for the followers of that religion. In the Christian church we will find the following symbols:

The cross – this represents the wooden cross that was used in Jesus' crucifixion. Where the figure of Jesus is shown on the cross, this is referred to as a crucifix. The death of Jesus is important to Christians as it reminds them that through Jesus' crucifixion, God's love for the world was shown. A plain cross reminds Christians that Jesus did not stay dead forever but rose from the dead.

The fish – this comes from the Greek word 'icthus'. Christians adopted this symbol many years ago when they were persecuted because of their beliefs. When a Christian met someone, they would draw an outline of a fish in the dirt on the ground. If the other person was a Christian, they would fill in the eye on the outline. It was a symbol that ensured that Christians knew who they could trust and who they couldn't.

The candle – used as a symbol of the presence of God. Christians believe that Jesus is the 'Light of the World'. Some Christians light a candle when praying to remind them that Jesus is near. When babies are baptised, they are given a lighted candle in the hope that when they grow up, they will share their belief in God with others.

The dove – in the story of Noah's ark, Noah sent out a dove to see if the flood had stopped and the world was ready for a fresh start. The dove is a symbol of the Holy Spirit for Christians.

The Chi Rho – made up of the first two Greek letters of the word Christ. The word 'Christ' means 'the chosen one'.

The Alpha Omega – made by using the first and last letters of the Greek alphabet. It is used to show the Christian belief that God was there at the beginning of time and will be there at the end of time.

Activities

Starting points	Light a candle – one of the symbols found in the church. Ask the children to look at the candle for no more than a few seconds, then to close their eyes and think about what Jesus means to Christians. ⚠️ **Supervise candles at all times.**
Worksheet 11 (Easy) *'Symbols'*	Ask the children to consider why symbols are important. Where do we find them and what do they mean? Why do we need them?
Worksheet 12 (Core) *'Symbols in the church'*	Look at some images of inside a church. See if the children can spot the symbols discussed during the lesson.
Worksheet 13 (Challenge) *'Symbol hunt'*	Discuss what symbols the children will see around school as they walk round with the CCA or adult helper.

Plenary

Ask the children to identify what the symbols around school mean by looking at the work produced by the challenge group. Are there any signs that should be in school that aren't?

Symbols

- Think about the symbols that you see in the environment. They may be on the road, on a piece of clothing or could represent a group. Draw some examples of symbols that you know and write about what they mean. We have given an example to help you.

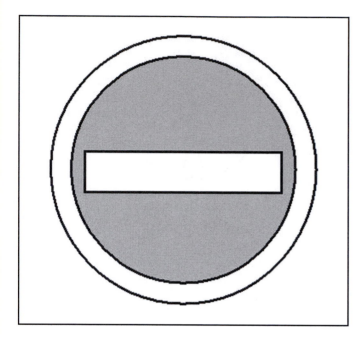

This sign means 'No entry'.

_____

_____

_____

_____

FOLENS RE IN ACTION 3 © Folens (copiable page)

Symbols in the church

● Cut out the symbols on the worksheet and stick them on a separate piece of paper. Write definitions for each, thinking about what they mean to Christians.

Symbol hunt

● Walk around your school noting which symbols and signs you can see. Record these on your worksheet as you walk around school. Remember to write down what the signs and symbols mean.

FOLENS RE IN ACTION 3

Rama and Sita

Learning objectives

Children should:
- learn about the key events and have an overview of the story of Rama and Sita
- consider the meaning behind the story
- explore the feelings and motivations of the characters in the story.

Background

Rama was the eldest son of King Dasharatha. Kaikeyi, one of the king's three wives, had saved his life when he was in danger so the king had granted her two wishes. When the time came for Rama to be crowned as king, Kaikeyi asked if her son, Bharat, could be crowned instead. She also asked for Rama and his wife, Sita, to be sent away to the forest for 14 years.

The king was very sad but kept his promise to his wife. Rama agreed to go to the forest as his father had asked. Sita could not bear to be parted from her husband so she said that she would accompany him. Rama's stepbrother, Lakshman, also joined them.

There were demons and wild animals in the forest. The king of the demons was called Ravana. Ravana's sister saw Rama and wanted to marry him but Rama refused, saying that he was already married. This made her angry and she tried to kill Sita. Lakshman cut off Ravana's sister's nose and ears as punishment.

Ravana sought revenge. He asked his uncle to change himself into a golden deer. When Sita saw the deer she wanted to keep it. Rama set off after the deer. When Rama did not return, Sita asked Lakshman to find him. Before he left, Lakshman drew a circle of protection around Sita and asked her to stay inside it. While Lakshman was away the evil Ravana disguised himself as a beggar asking for food. Sita stepped out of the circle to try and find him some food and as soon as she did this, Ravana grabbed her and took her away to his magic kingdom of Lanka. Ravana tried to persuade Sita to marry him but she refused.

It was not long before Rama and Lakshman realised that they had been tricked. They began searching for Sita. Rama asked the king of the monkeys, Hanuman, for help. Hanuman gathered an army and they set off to find Sita. After a long battle, Sita was rescued. Rama defeated the ten-headed demon, Ravana, by using a special bow and arrow.

After 14 years Rama, Sita and Lakshman returned to Ayodha, their home. They were welcomed back by people lighting rows of clay lamps, which they placed in their windows. Celebrations were held and Rama was crowned king. The story of Rama's victory over Ravana is a celebration of the victory of good over evil.

Activities

Starting points	Make a timeline of the key events in the story of 'Rama and Sita'.
Worksheet 14 (Easy) *'Hanuman mask'*	Explore the methods that the children could use for designing a mask. Will it be one that fixes to their head or will it be one that they can move about? What materials will they use?
Worksheet 15 (Core) *'Wanted!'*	Discuss the best methods for trying to catch Ravana. How could he be trapped?
Worksheet 16 (Challenge) *'Please, Ravana!'*	Explore the feelings Sita may have experienced when she was a prisoner of the evil Ravana.

Plenary

Think about all the characters that you have heard about in the story of Rama and Sita. How did the characters differ and how were they similar? What were their personalities like?

Hanuman mask

● Use the sheet to design a Hanuman mask. Think about what materials you are going to use. How will you attach it to your head?

Wanted!

- Imagine that the evil Ravana has escaped and you have been asked to try to catch him. You need some help. Design a wanted poster describing what he is wanted for and what he looks like. Don't forget the reward!

Please, Ravana!

● Imagine you are Sita and the evil Ravana has captured you. Write a letter to Ravana pleading with him to let you go. How could you appeal to his better nature?

_____

_____

_____

_____

_____

_____

_____

_____

_____

Celebrating Divali

Learning objectives

Children should:
- identify some of the customs and practices related to celebrating Divali
- learn about the symbolic significance of a diva and how it relates to the Divali story
- know about the importance of preparation for Divali.

Background

The word Divali comes from the word Deepavali, which means, 'row of lights'. The festival of Divali can last for up to five days. The most important reason why Hindus celebrate Divali is to celebrate the triumph of good over evil. It is a time for renewing hopes for happiness and prosperity in life. Hindus believe that the god Vishnu protects the world with his goodness and that he comes to earth in many forms to challenge evil. These different forms are called avatars and they are accompanied by goddesses, who supply extra energy. At Divali, stories are told about Vishnu and his wife, Lakshmi, and about Krishna, Rama and Sita.

On the first evening of Divali, many Hindus will light a single lamp (a diva) and place it in front of the house. It acts as a reminder to Hindus that death is a part of life. An image of Lakshmi is carefully washed in milk. These murtis (the word to describe images of gods or goddesses) are treated with great respect and are used as part of daily worship to help worshippers concentrate on God. The washing of the murti acts as a reminder to Hindus to aim for pure thoughts and deeds in their lives. The first day is also a time for eating sweets made from thickened milk.

The second day celebrates the victory of the god Krishna over the demon Narakasur. Men rub their bodies with perfumed oils before bathing. Afterwards, clean or new clothes are worn. A large breakfast is eaten, often with friends or relatives. Fireworks are set off in the morning and evening. Special sweet dishes are also eaten as part of the midday meal.

On the third day, divas are lit to invite the goddess Lakshmi into their homes. Hindus hope that Lakshmi's visit will bring good fortune, good health and happiness. Rangoli patterns are drawn at the entrance of houses to welcome the goddess.

On the last day of the year, houses are cleaned from top to bottom. It is believed that Lakshmi will bless clean homes. The front door is decorated with a garland or piece of cloth, called a toran. Greeting cards are sent around the world. The cards have images of gods or goddesses on them. Accounts are settled and a special ceremony is carried out in the hope that Lakshmi will bring prosperity during the coming year.

On the fourth day of Divali, new clothes are worn and presents are given. Friends and relatives are visited and gifts of food are exchanged. Hindus visit the mandir and food offerings are made to the murtis. After a special ceremony, the food is shared out among the worshippers. On the fifth day of Divali, married men do not eat any food cooked by their wives. Instead they visit their sisters, who give them a delicious meal to eat.

Activities

Starting points	Recap the story of Rama and Sita.
Worksheet 17 (Easy) *'A new outfit for Divali'*	Look at some images of Hindus celebrating Divali. Ask the children to design a new outfit for the celebrations on the worksheet.
Worksheet 18 (Mixed ability) *'Divali celebrations'*	Recap what Hindus do to celebrate Divali. Ask the children to produce details of these in a leaflet.

Plenary

Light a diva. Write a list of emotions on the board that Hindus may experience during Divali.

A new outfit for Divali

- Imagine that you are celebrating Divali. You want to look your best! Design a new outfit, making sure that it is bright and colourful.

Divali celebrations

- Design a leaflet for the celebration of Divali, perhaps similar to the one in the picture. Include details of everything that Hindus do to celebrate the festival.

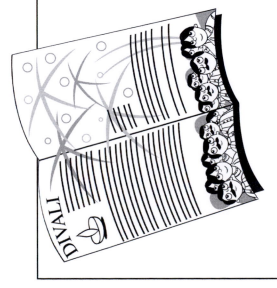

DIVALI

Lakshmi

Learning objectives

Children should:
- learn that some Hindus worship Lakshmi, the goddess of wealth
- understand that Hindus believe that the many qualities of God are represented in various ways
- know that Divali is the start of the new year for Hindus.

Background

Whenever Vishnu comes down to earth, Lakshmi takes the form of his wife. She represents Vishnu's divine energy and power. In one story, it is said that she came to earth standing on a lotus flower.

Lakshmi was created from an ocean of milk. She is seen to be pure, just as a lotus flower floating on water is not spoilt by the muddy soil from which it grows. The washing of a murti of Lakshmi on the first day of Divali acts as a reminder to Hindus to aim for pure thoughts and deeds in their lives.

Lakshmi represents good fortune, wealth and beauty. Hindus invite the goddess to enter their homes so that they are blessed with good health, happiness and good fortune. Divas are lit to welcome the goddess.

Pictures of Lakshmi show her standing or sitting on a lotus flower. She has four hands, which show her different qualities and powers. In two of her hands she carries lotus flowers, which are signs of purity and perfection. The third hand, with an upraised palm, is a sign of Lakshmi offering her worshippers protection from evil. Gold coins fall from her fourth hand. This is a sign of Lakshmi's power to bring riches and prosperity to those who worship her with purity and unselfishness in their hearts.

Another way of welcoming Lakshmi into the home is by drawing rangoli patterns on the floor of the entrance to each house. A rangoli is a sign of welcome. Some Hindus draw one daily as a sign to welcome guests. The patterns are made with fingers using flour, rice, grains or coloured chalk and are square, rectangular or circular in shape. They include geometric patterns and sometimes lotus flowers.

Activities

Starting points	Recap the other ways in which Hindus celebrate Divali.
Worksheet 19 (Easy) *'Rangoli patterns'*	Look at examples of rangoli patterns. Ask the children to draw one of their own on the worksheet.
Worksheet 20 (Core) *'New Year resolutions'*	Make a list of common New Year resolutions that people make. How quickly are these broken?
Worksheet 21 (Challenge) *'Hindu gods'*	Make a list of the Hindu gods and goddesses encountered so far in the work on Hinduism.

Plenary

Hindus decorate their doorsteps with rangoli patterns to welcome the goddess Lakshmi into their homes. Ask the children to consider how they make visitors to their homes feel welcome.

Rangoli patterns

- Design your own rangoli pattern, making it as bright and colourful as you can. You can either draw a circular, square or rectangular shape.

New Year resolutions

● Make a list of the resolutions that you think you should make. Try to be as honest as you can but don't choose ones that are going to be difficult to keep! One has been given to start you off.

1. I will keep my bedroom tidy!

2. _____

_____

3. _____

_____

4. _____

_____

FOLENS RE IN ACTION 3   © Folens (copiable page)

Hindu gods

● Now research the other gods and goddesses within Hinduism. Draw a picture of two of them, find out what their qualities are and think about what they have done to make themselves important or well-known.

Jesus

Learning objectives

Children should:
- learn that Jesus was a historical figure
- know that there is no authentic visual image of Jesus
- reflect on their own ideas of how Jesus may have looked.

Background

Christians believe in the teachings of Jesus, who they also call Christ. The word 'Christian' means 'a follower of Christ'. Christians believe that Jesus is God's son and that Jesus' death was a sign of God's love for the world.

Jesus was born approximately two thousand years ago in the town of Bethlehem. Little was known about him until he reached the age of thirty, when he asked his cousin, John the Baptist, to baptise him in the River Jordan. After his baptism, Jesus went into the desert for forty days and forty nights. While he was there, the devil tried to tempt him but Jesus refused all the offers that the devil made.

One of the most important talks that Jesus gave was called the Sermon on the Mount. During this time, he blessed groups of people and stated the laws that people should follow. He also taught through parables, which are stories that contain a meaning.

However, Jesus became unpopular three years after he started teaching. It was hoped that Jesus would establish a new Jewish kingdom but when it became clear that he was not going to do this, the people turned against him.

Jesus knew he was going to die and shared a Last Supper with his disciples. Judas, one of Jesus' disciples, betrayed him and Jesus was taken to see Pontius Pilate, the Roman governor. Although he did not want Jesus to be killed, he was worried that the Jews would turn against him and he ordered that Jesus should die through crucifixion. However, on the third day after Jesus' death, his tomb was found to be empty. News quickly spread that he had risen from the dead.

Activities

Starting points	Although we have several stories about Jesus, we do not know what he looked like. Look at a range of images of Jesus, both modern and traditional.
Worksheet 22 (Easy) *'Friends'*	Ask the children to consider what makes a good friend. What qualities should they have?
Worksheet 23 (Core) *'Images of Jesus'*	Ask the children to sort the images of Jesus into ones that they don't like and ones that they do.
Worksheet 24 (Challenge) *'Jesus in art'*	Ask the children to think about what qualities the images of Jesus portray and ask them to discuss with a partner which of the images they prefer.

Plenary

Discuss why Jesus was portrayed in different ways.

NOTE: Muslim children must not be asked to draw images of Jesus.

Friends

- Draw a picture of a classmate and then describe their qualities. See if the other children in the class can guess who the person is by the written description only.

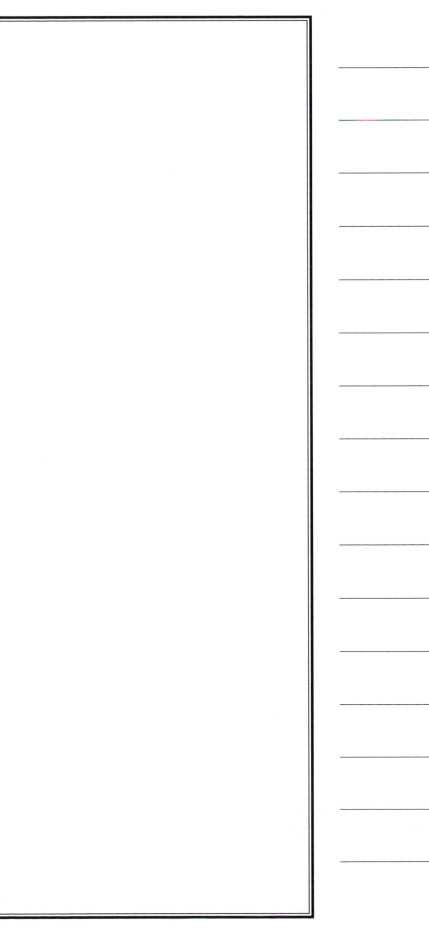

_____

_____

_____

_____

_____

_____

_____

_____

_____

_____

_____

_____

Images of Jesus

- Think about all the images you have seen of Jesus. Describe how you think Jesus looked. If your religion allows it, draw a picture of Jesus to illustrate your description.

Jesus in art

● Look at a range of pictures of Jesus. Choose your favourite picture and then, if your religion allows, reproduce it. Write about why you prefer this picture to the others you have looked at.

What was Jesus like?

Learning objectives

Children should:
- understand what the Gospels tell us about what Jesus was like
- summarise from the evidence what sort of person Jesus was.

Background

One day Jesus was speaking to a large crowd of people when Jairus, one of the rulers of the synagogue, came to speak to him.

He fell at Jesus' feet crying; "My daughter is dying! Please come and see her so that she will be well again."

Jesus started to walk with him but a large crowd started to gather around. A woman who had been poorly for many years touched Jesus' cloak as he passed. She believed that if she could touch him she would be healed. Immediately, she felt a lot better and realised that she had been cured.

Jesus realised that all his power had left him. He turned around and asked, "Who touched my clothes?" No one answered, so Jesus kept looking around to see who had touched him. The old woman eventually came up to him and confessed. Jesus told her that it was her faith in him that had cured her.

While Jesus had been speaking to the woman, some people from the house of Jairus arrived. They told him that Jairus' daughter was dead.

Jesus ignored what they said and asked his disciples, Peter, James and John, to follow him to the house of the little girl. Her father followed behind, crying and distraught.

When Jesus arrived at the house, he told the girl's family that she was not dead but merely asleep. They all laughed at him.

He asked the child's family to leave and, one by one, they did.

He took the girl by the hand and said, "Talitha koum!" meaning, "Little girl, I say to you, get up!" Immediately, the girl stood up and walked around the room, much to the astonishment of her relatives who had been waiting outside.

Jesus left the house with the disciples after asking Jairus to give his daughter something to eat and not to tell anyone about the story.

Activities

Starting points	Think about what we have learned about Jesus from this story. Put yourself in the position of the people around him. Would you want to know Jesus? Would you want to be his friend?
Worksheet 25 (Easy) *'Postcard home'*	Make a list of adjectives with the children to describe the feelings of a person in the crowd.
Worksheet 26 (Core) *'Interview of a disciple'*	Discuss what questions the children could ask a disciple.
Worksheet 27 (Challenge) *'It happened here…'*	Discuss the main events of the story with the children. What important things would they need to include in a newspaper report?

Plenary

Explore the qualities that Jesus must have possessed to be able to perform miracles.

Postcard home

● Imagine that you are staying in the area where Jesus has performed the miracle of Jairus' daughter. Write a postcard home to a friend explaining what you witnessed when Jesus cured the woman in the crowd and then when you heard about Jesus bringing Jairus' daughter back to life.

Interview of a disciple

● Pretend that you have been asked to interview one of the disciples present at the scene of the miracle of Jairus' daughter. Write a list of questions that you would want to ask.

1. _____

_____

2. _____

_____

3. _____

_____

4. _____

_____

It happened here...

● Write a newspaper report based on the miracle of Jairus' daughter. Include a headline and a picture. Try to describe the emotions of those involved in the story.

Mary Jones

Learning objective

Children should:
- understand that the Bible is a sacred/holy book which forms the basis of the Christian faith.

Background

Mary Jones lived in a small cottage in the Welsh countryside many years ago. One day, as she walked to the nearest village with her parents, she was excited to see that a new school would be opening.

Mary hoped that this would mean that she could learn to read the Bible. There was only one problem; she did not own a Bible and her parents were too poor to buy her one.

Mary saved and saved until at last she had enough money to be able to afford a Bible. She had been told that there was a man in a town called Bala who would have one to sell her. However, the town was over 20 miles away.

Mary set off early one morning. She crossed many streams, followed many paths and walked through many valleys, until she eventually found the house where the gentleman lived.

Mr Charles was astonished when he realised how far Mary had walked. He was pleased that she had arrived when she did as he only had one Bible left. Mary took the Bible and travelled back home.

It was some months later, at a meeting in London, when Mr Charles shared the story of Mary Jones with some important men. It was one of the many stories like Mary's that led the Bible Society, which distributes Bibles to those in need, to be set up in 1804.

Activities

Starting points	Mary Jones travelled a long way for her Bible. Discuss with the children what sacrifices they would be prepared to make so that they could achieve or acquire something that they longed for.
Worksheet 28 (Easy) *'Preparations'*	Ask the children to consider the journey that Mary Jones went on. Would they be able to make that journey now?
Worksheet 29 (Core) *'Which way now?'*	Look at some different types of maps to see which common features you can see on all of them.
Worksheet 30 (Challenge) *'Journeys'*	Discuss what you see on the way into school in the morning.

Plenary

Let the challenge group research and report back on what the role of the Bible Society is today. How does it differ from the society that was set up many years ago?

Preparations

● Imagine that you are Mary Jones. Think about what you would put in your picnic basket to prepare you for your long journey. Would you need an extra jumper if it goes cold? Make sure you include enough food and drink. Make a list and draw pictures of some of the items you have included.

FOLENS RE IN ACTION 3   43

Which way now?

- Draw an imaginary map for Mary Jones. Make sure you include the valleys, streams and rivers that she passed on her way. What else did she see?

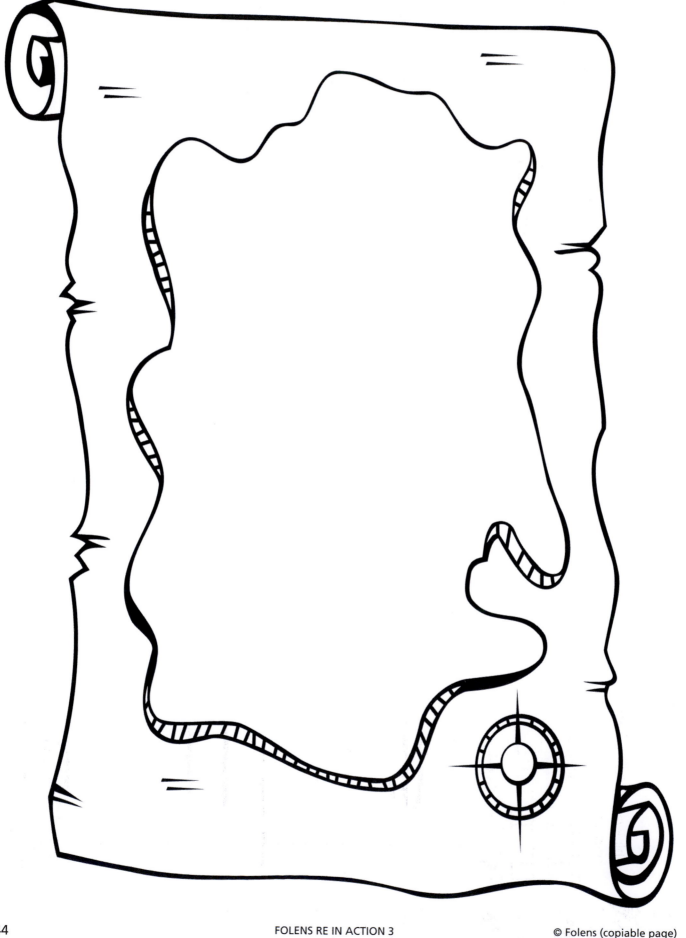

Journeys

30

- Think about the journey on your way to school. What would be the similarities and differences between your journey and Mary Jones' journey to the town of Bala?

Similarities	Differences
Journey to Bala	Journey to school

Old Testament/New Testament

Learning objectives

Children should:
- know about the composition of the Bible and its variety
- learn about the differences between the Old and New Testaments.

Background

The Bible is divided into the Old Testament and New Testament. Another word for testament is promise. Christians use the Bible for worship and for help during difficult times. It acts as a guide for life.

The Old Testament was written in Hebrew. There are 39 books in the Old Testament. It tells the story of the creation, the history of Jews and the relationship between Jews and God.

The New Testament was written in Greek. It tells of the life of Jesus. It teaches that salvation comes through the belief that Jesus died and went to heaven. The New Testament is made up of four gospels, 21 epistles, and two other books called Acts and Revelations.

Gospel means 'good news'. Matthew, Mark, Luke and John wrote the gospels. Each gospel tells of the life, death and resurrection of Jesus from its author's viewpoint.

Acts looks at the development of Christianity after the resurrection of Jesus.

An epistle is a letter. A man called Paul, who became a Christian, wrote most of them after the death of Jesus. He gave encouragement to the early Christians.

Revelation is the final book in the New Testament and describes what will happen at the end of time.

Activities

Starting points	Discuss what skills the children need to find specific books in the Bible.
Worksheet 31 (Easy) *'Bible wordsearch'*	Recap how to find words in a wordsearch.
Worksheet 32 (Core) *'Books! Books! Books!'*	Look at a list of the books found in the Bible. Identify any difficult names.
Worksheet 33 (Challenge) *'Who's who?'*	Talk about some of the most important characters in the Bible.

Plenary

Ask the children in the core group to read out the names of the books found in the Bible.

Bible wordsearch

● Find the books of the New Testament listed below in the wordsearch puzzle. Cross the name out when you have found it.

Matthew	Luke
John	Acts
Romans	Corinthians
Colossians	Timothy
Titus	Philemon
Hebrews	James
Peter	Galatians
Jude	Revelation

P	H	I	L	E	M	O	N	Y	T	U	I	C
N	O	I	T	A	L	E	V	E	R	H	P	O
C	R	S	M	A	T	T	H	E	W	E	L	L
X	O	P	S	D	J	L	I	K	V	B	K	O
O	T	R	L	M	U	B	O	U	C	R	V	S
P	I	B	I	N	D	C	T	L	D	E	B	S
S	M	R	O	N	E	I	N	Z	S	W	N	I
T	O	V	J	I	T	W	E	H	R	S	S	A
Q	T	O	Y	U	G	H	S	W	O	I	E	N
W	H	A	S	T	Y	H	I	T	M	J	M	S
N	Y	S	W	Q	C	V	R	A	A	G	A	S
S	N	A	I	T	A	L	A	G	N	F	J	D
P	E	T	E	R	B	A	C	T	S	S	V	C

Books! Books! Books!

- The list of books from the Bible has been scrambled up. Use the Bible as a reference and try to unscramble the books. We have done one for you.

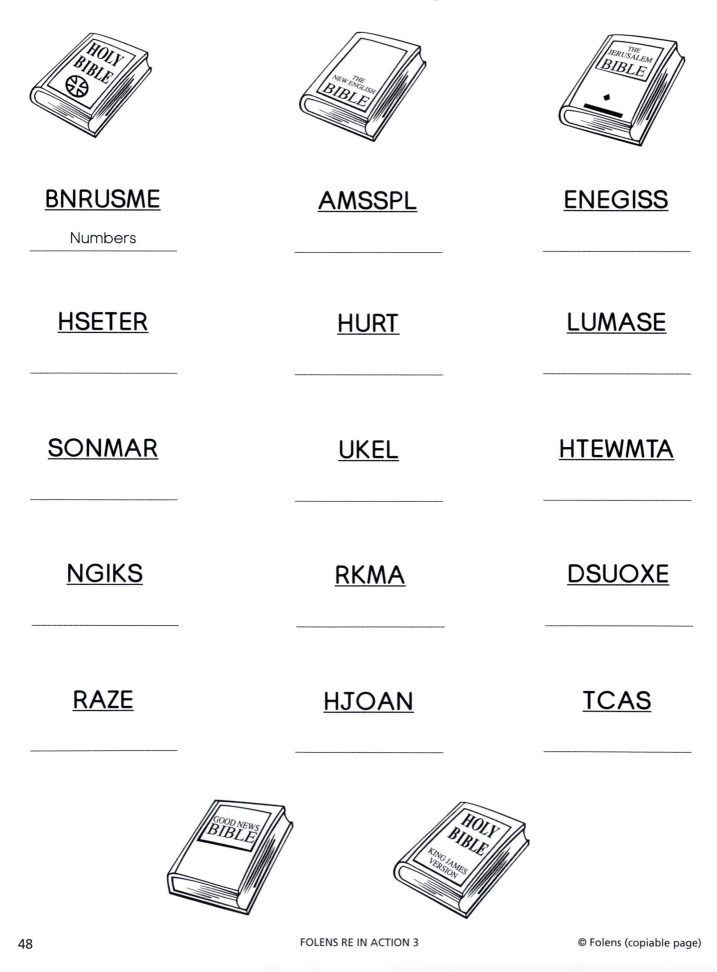

BNRUSME

Numbers

AMSSPL

_____

ENEGISS

_____

HSETER

_____

HURT

_____

LUMASE

_____

SONMAR

_____

UKEL

_____

HTEWMTA

_____

NGIKS

_____

RKMA

_____

DSUOXE

_____

RAZE

_____

HJOAN

_____

TCAS

_____

Who's who?

● Use a Bible to find out about one of the central characters in the Bible. Think about what they did, whether they had any family, if they knew Jesus and what type of person they were. Examples you could choose from are Eve, Moses, Esther, Samson and Joseph, son of Jacob. Draw a picture of what you imagine they looked like and list some information about them.

Bible writing

Learning objectives

Children should:
- know about the composition of the Bible and its variety
- learn about the differences between the Old and New Testaments.

Background

There are different types of writing in the Bible. The books in the Old Testament are divided into law, history, poetry and wisdom, and prophets.

Law

These books describe the origins of the Jewish people. They include stories about the Creation, the Exodus of the Jews from slavery in Egypt, laws about how Israelites should worship, the Jews' time in the desert and the speeches given to them by Moses when they were about to enter the Promised Land.

History

These books are concerned with the history of the Israelites. They are concerned with the death of Moses, the appointment of new leaders, the saving of the Jews by Esther and the rebuilding of the Temple.

Poetry and wisdom

These books contain the prayers and poems that think about human emotion. They also contain a collection of wise sayings.

Prophets

These include predictions about future events. However, their main task was to call God's people back to Him.

The books in the New Testament are divided into Gospels and Acts, Letters and Revelation.

Gospels and Acts

The word gospel means 'good news'. The Gospels emphasise the events of the last week of Jesus' life, his death and his resurrection. Matthew looks at Jesus as the Messiah, long expected by the Jews; Mark looks at Jesus' life and work; Luke emphasises Jesus as the saviour of the poor and needy and John looks at the miracles he performed. Acts examines the time after Jesus' ascension into heaven.

Letters

The church was helped in its early years by apostles who wrote letters teaching about God and the gospel, including instructions on how to live life as a Christian.

Revelation

This book focuses upon a series of predictions about a new heaven and a new earth.

Activities

Starting points	Discuss the different books found in the school library. Compare these to the different types of book found in the Bible.
Worksheet 34 (Mixed ability) *'Bible books'*	Recap the skills needed to find specific books in the Bible.
Worksheet 35 (Challenge) *'New Testament cover'*	Look at a range of different Bibles and use them to identify some Bible stories with the children.

Plenary

Ask the children in the challenge group to read out the names of the characters in the story that they researched for their Bible cover.

Bible books

● With a partner, find the books listed below in the Bible. Write what page you have found the book on and copy out a quote from the Bible.

Name of book: MARK

Page number:

Quote:

Name of book: ACTS

Page number:

Quote:

Name of book: LUKE

Page number:

Quote:

Name of book: JOHN

Page number:

Quote:

Name of book: ROMANS

Page number:

Quote:

Name of book: MATTHEW

Page number:

Quote:

New Testament cover

- Design a cover for the New Testament. Research a story that you could use as a basis for the cover using some children's Bibles.

FOLENS RE IN ACTION 3

© Folens (copiable page)

Hagar

Learning objective

Children should:
- understand what the word 'faith' means in a religious sense.

Background

Sarah was Abraham's wife. After many years of waiting to have a child, she began to feel disappointed and impatient. She wondered whether she would ever become the mother of Abraham's child.

Hagar was Abraham's and Sarah's slave. Women sold into slavery had no rights. They could be given to the head of the household to secure the birth of the male heir. This child then would not belong to its mother but to her owner. Sarah and Abraham took the decision to let Hagar have a baby for them.

When Hagar realised that she was having Abraham's baby, she began to think of herself as important and started to treat Sarah differently. When Sarah complained to Abraham, he told her to treat Hagar how she liked, reminding her that Hagar was the slave.

Eventually, Hagar ran away. When she stopped to rest at a spring in the desert, an angel of God appeared. The angel explained that God had realised that she was unhappy, but that she should go back to Sarah and obey her and that she would have a son called Ishmael.

Hagar was pleased that God had noticed her unhappiness. She went back to Sarah and had a baby, which she named Ishmael.

Activities

Starting points	Explore what we mean by the word 'faith'. What does it mean to have faith? How do people show others that they have religious faith? What actions do they carry out and what do they believe?
Worksheet 36 (Easy) *'Slave needed...'*	Make a list of the jobs that people in school do and what each job entails.
Worksheet 37 (Core) *'Hagar's diary'*	Discuss what it would be like to be a slave. How would the children feel at being ordered about?
Worksheet 38 (Challenge) *'A problem shared...'*	Discuss why people used to have slaves. Was it the right thing to do?

Plenary

Discuss possible solutions to Hagar's dilemma. What could she do if she lived in a modern society?

Slave needed…

- Hagar ran into the desert to escape from Abraham and Sarah. While she was away, they needed a new slave. What qualities would they ask for? What would the new slave be needed to do? Write an advert for a new slave, including all of these details.

SLAVE NEEDED

FOLENS RE IN ACTION 3 © Folens (copiable page)

Hagar's diary

● Imagine what a day in Hagar's life was like. What jobs would she be expected to do? How did Abraham and Sarah treat her? Write a diary for a day, making sure that you include what she did during the day but, more importantly, the feelings she experienced.

DAY:

6.00 am

9.00 am

12.00 noon

3.00 pm

6.00 pm

9.00 pm

12.00 midnight

A problem shared...

- Imagine the dilemma that Hagar is in. She is not being treated well by her employers, she is having a baby and she has very little money. What could she do? Write a letter from Hagar to a problem page, explaining her situation.

FOLENS RE IN ACTION 3
© Folens (copiable page)

Sarah

Learning objective

Children should:
- explore the characteristics of faithfulness.

Background

As Abraham sat at his tent one day he saw three men close by. He hurried out to meet them, saying that he was honoured that they had come to his home and offered them water to wash their feet and food for their journey.

The men agreed and Abraham asked Sarah to bake some fresh bread. One of the men suddenly asked Abraham where Sarah was. Abraham explained that she was in the tent.

This man was really God. He told Abraham that when he returned in nine months, Sarah would have a son.

Sarah overheard what they were saying and laughed. She knew that she was far too old to have children.

God asked Abraham why Sarah had laughed. God said that nothing was too difficult for Him and that in nine months Sarah would have a son.

Sarah was embarrassed and lied that she had not laughed. Nine months later, Sarah gave birth to a baby boy. They named their son Isaac, which means, 'he laughs' - because Sarah had laughed.

Activities

Starting points	Invite children to think about where people put their faith today. Explore where the children put their faith, focusing on their idols: for example, football players or singers.
Worksheet 39 (Easy) 'Faithfulness'	Explore the reasons why Sarah may not have had faith in God.
Worksheet 40 (Core) 'Qualities'	Ask the children to contrast the characteristics of Abraham with their idol. It could be a famous singer or football player or they may choose someone else. What qualities do each of the people have?
Worksheet 41 (Challenge) 'Faithful'	Make a list of the people that children put their faith into today. Contrast these with where you put your faith when you were a similar age. Can you have faith in everyone you meet?

Plenary

Explore the meaning of the word 'faithful'.

Faithfulness

- Think about someone whom you have faith in. How do you know that you can trust them and that they will not let you down? Draw a picture of them and then describe them.

Qualities

● Contrast the characteristics of Abraham with your idol. It could be a famous singer or football player, or you may choose someone else. What qualities do each of the people have? We have given one to help you.

Abraham

1. Trustworthy _____
2. _____
3. _____
4. _____
5. _____
6. _____
7. _____
8. _____
9. _____
10. _____
11. _____
12. _____

My idol: _____

1. _____
2. _____
3. _____
4. _____
5. _____
6. _____
7. _____
8. _____
9. _____
10. _____
11. _____
12. _____

Faithful

● Consider people that you know whom you consider faithful. What qualities do they have and how do they behave? Draw a picture of them and make a list of these qualities.

Qualities

Abraham

Learning objectives

Children should:
- learn about the story of Abraham
- reflect on the emotional impact of the story.

Background

God knew Abraham for his faithfulness and obedience. God had promised Abraham that he would have many descendants and that they would become a great nation. Abraham knew that God would do as He promised.

One day, God decided to test Abraham's faith. He told Abraham to take Isaac, his son, to a mountain and offer him as a sacrifice.

Although Abraham must have felt very upset at the thought of losing his precious son, he trusted God and set off the following morning to the land of Moriah with Isaac and two servants.

On the third day, Abraham saw the mountain that God had described in the distance, so he set off with Isaac, a knife and some wood for the fire. Isaac questioned where the sacrificial lamb was but Abraham told him that he trusted that God would provide it.

When they arrived, Abraham built an altar of stones and wood. He took Isaac, tied his arms together and laid him on the altar. He took the knife and tried to summon the courage to kill Isaac.

Suddenly, an angel appeared. The angel told Abraham that he had passed the test and that he knew Abraham truly loved God, as he had been prepared to sacrifice his son for Him.

Abraham was so relieved that when he saw a nearby ram caught in a bush he offered it as a sacrifice to God. Abraham and Isaac then returned home to Sarah and Hagar.

Activities

Starting points	Recap the three stories about the characters of Abraham, Sarah and Hagar.
Worksheet 42 (Easy) *'Character profile'*	Discuss with the children everything they know about Abraham.
Worksheet 43 (Core) *'In the hot seat'*	Discuss the three characters of Abraham, Sarah and Hagar. Make a list of their qualities. Who was wrong? Who was right?
Worksheet 44 (Challenge) *'Abraham'*	Ask the children to think carefully about the story of Abraham and to list the separate main components of the story.

Plenary

Choose three children to be the characters of Abraham, Sarah and Hagar. Ask the core children in the class to read out their questions and the three chosen children will answer in role.

Character profile

- Create a character profile for Abraham. Include details such as his age, who he was married to, a photo and details of his friends.

Name: _____

Address: _____

_____

_____

_____

Age: _____

Eye colour: _____

Hair colour: _____

Job: _____

Personality:

_____

_____

_____

_____

_____

Family:

_____

_____

_____

_____

_____

In the hot seat

- Now that you have heard about the characters of Abraham, Sarah and Hagar, make a list of the questions that you would like to ask them if they were alive today. Remember that you want to explore the feelings of the characters as they carried out the actions that they did.

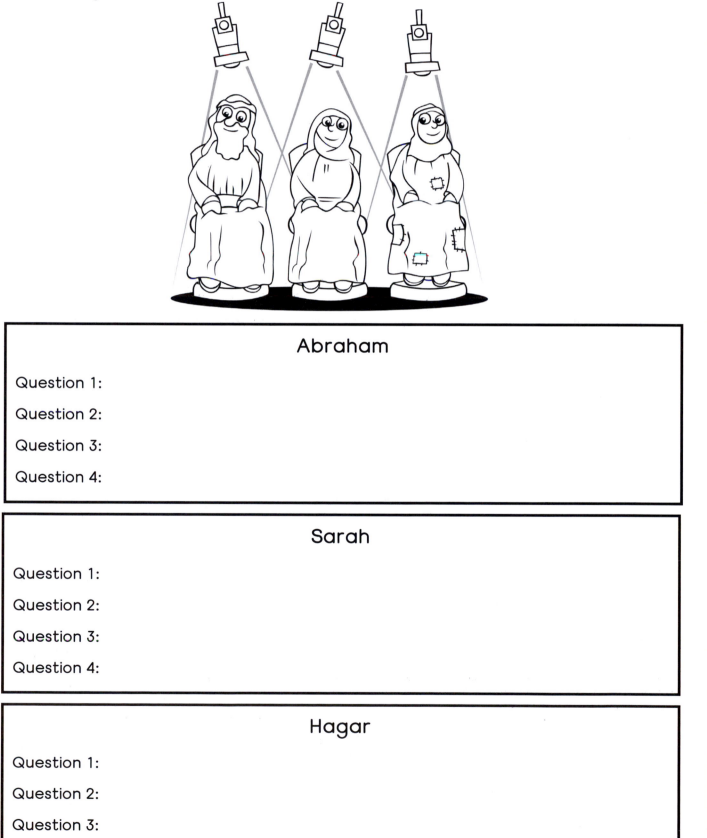

Abraham

Question 1:

Question 2:

Question 3:

Question 4:

Sarah

Question 1:

Question 2:

Question 3:

Question 4:

Hagar

Question 1:

Question 2:

Question 3:

Question 4:

Abraham

Create an acrostic poem for Abraham, thinking about his actions and what type of person he was. The first line has been completed for you.

 sked to sacrifice his son by God.

 _____

 _____

 _____

 _____

h _____

a _____

m _____

FOLENS RE IN ACTION 3   © Folens (copiable page)